UNKNOWN DORSET

Alison Poole and Michael Williams

BOSSINEY BOOKS

First published in 1989 by
Bossiney Books
St Teath, Bodmin, Cornwall.

Typeset and Printed by
Clowes Book Printers
St Columb, Cornwall.

Bound by R Booth (Bookbinders) Ltd
Mabe Burnthouse, Cornwall

ISBN 0 948158 55 7

PLATE ACKNOWLEDGMENTS

Cover photography by Dorset Media Services
Back cover by Ray Bishop

Ray Bishop: pages 5, 7, 8, 11, 12, 13, 14, 18, 21, 23, 24, 26, 27, 28, 33, 34, 41, 55, 56, 57, 59, 61, 63, 79, 81, 83, 94

Trevor Kenward: pages 3, 10, 31, 38, 42, 43, 44, 45, 50, 51, 65, 64, 66, 69

Felicity Young: page 39

Parnham House: pages 47, 48

Alec R Thirkettle: page 17

Alison Poole: pages 19, 70, 71, 73, 74, 75, 76, 84, 85, 86, 87, 88, 90, 91, 92, 93

Paul Yockney: page 53

About the author
MICHAEL WILLIAMS

A Cornishman, Michael Williams started full-time publishing in 1975. With his wife Sonia, he runs Bossiney Books from a cottage and converted barn in North Cornwall – they are literally cottage publishers. Bossiney now publishes in six regions: Dorset, Wiltshire, Avon, Somerset, Devon and Cornwall. This is their fourth Dorset title. Michael makes several visits to Dorset each year.

In addition to publishing and writing, Michael Williams is a keen cricket enthusiast and collector of cricket books. President of the Cornish Crusaders Cricket Club and a member of the Cornwall and Gloucestershire County Clubs, he recalls that the first county match he watched involved Dorset. He is also Vice-President of the Cornwall Rugby Football Union.

A member of the RSPCA, Michael has worked for reform in laws relating to animal welfare. In 1984, he was elected a member of The Ghost Club, and his most recent book in this field is 'Supernatural Adventure' in which he investigates automatic writing, time travel, ghost hunting, UFOs, hand analysis and water divining.

Michael Williams

A Bossiney milestone: celebration cake for photographer Ray Bishop marking his 1,000th photograph for Bossiney. Left to right: publishers Michael and Sonia Williams, Ray Bishop and Westcountry author and journalist Sarah Foot.

Unknown Dorset

'Unknown Dorset.'

Can there be truly such a place?

Despite improved communications and the growth of tourism, we believe the answer is 'Yes!' It is almost as if Dorset wears a kind of cloak. The truth is a surprising number of people like discovering for themselves. They distrust guide-books. They resent being side-tracked and told what they ought to see.

'Relatively Unknown Dorset' may have been a more accurate title, yet curiously, in Dorset today, you can still get off the beaten track, and some parts of the county tenaciously retain ancient secrets. It is this unique spirit that we have tried to pin to paper in words and illustrations.

Before we begin trekking across these pages – and Dorset itself: a sentence or two of warning. A good deal depends on how we define that word 'unknown,' and remember writers can be strange characters. The great G K Chesterton, in a depressed condition, cheered himself up by reading a book called *Funeral Customs: Their Origin and Development.* He found the subject of death and burial brightened him – lifted his spirit. Life itself can be an enigma, for the same Mr Chesterton reflected on another occasion: 'If you leave a thing alone you leave it to a torrent of change. If you leave a white post alone, it will soon be a black post.'

Tracing the distant history of Dorset can be difficult, like reading a book whose pages grow blurred and confused as the plot unfolds.

The earliest evidence of human activity in the county we know

A secret corner of Dorset.

today as Dorset comes from the Old Stone Age. During that time of relative warmth between the Ice Ages, traces of that human activity have come to us through flint tools found in places like Sherborne and Corfe Mullen.

The mists, of course, have gone thinner with the passing of each century. To such an extent that our presentday archaeologist, with modern techniques of excavation and radiocarbon dating, can answer some of our questions with a degree of certainty.

Yet oddly enough sections of the county remain a secret country. We find beautiful churches almost hidden in delightful countryside, and many of these churches and rectories hold secrets – not just all those confessions – though they would contain masses of astonishing facts and admissions, enough to fill a thousand books.

And in this century the Army has created its own secret landscapes where time has somehow halted under gunfire and necessary training. Lulworth is such a case, and it is intriguing to reflect that future generations, with a sense of curiosity, will turn to these military areas to see what our Britain of the late twentieth century looked like.

A deep sense of the past undoubtedly broods over Dorset.

No county has a greater literary tradition. There are romantic links with historic happenings. King Alfred loved Dorset; as did Sir Walter Raleigh who called it 'Dorset Dear' and resolved to end his earthly days here. 'It is impossible not to love it,' said Arthur Mee when he toured the county in the late 1930s, 'It is one of the corners of England for which we all feel something like affection.'

Life was going on in Dorset in those dim, dark centuries before the Romans came. Even today in many corners of the county you

The Church of St Laurence at Upwey near Weymouth. Christianity reached Upwey some 1,000 years ago when the Saxons founded a little chantry here close to the holy well. The church is a delight with its mellow stone, yew trees and ancient gravestones. Inside there are rare wall paintings which have been carefully uncovered from their coating of whitewash.

Few parts of England can compare with Dorset's charm.

have this strong sense of historic continuity stretching back to a distant past. Moreover few other parts of England can compare with Dorset's charm and beauty: the loveliness and sheer variety of its landscape, the attractive villages, the manor houses, the cottages and the farms – mellow stone, the brick and the thatch and, above all, those gardens – some small, others medium-sized to large – that could only belong to 'Dorsetshire'.

Often here you find yourself looking downward – not into a wide world but into a hollow. Often too in that hollow there is silence, admittedly a very positive silence, and no movement, except perhaps for some sheep quietly grazing. Then, in contrast, you can be on the crest of downland and see whole chunks of Dorset, Somerset and Wiltshire merging to make lines of colour and Westcountry life. Dorset can make you feel oddly vulnerable: shades subtle and motives vague, mysteriously unsure like twilight in a strange land or waking from a deep sleep. Much depends on the mood and the moment.

Dorset is strong in folklore – so powerful in fact that it has become part of the countryside and the coastline. Paradox is everywhere – this mysterious mingling of history and legend. And beyond that lies the inevitable question: 'Can there be such a thing as total myth?'

If we could climb aboard on some magical time machine and go back into the past – to Abbotsbury – we should on the thirteenth day of May encounter an ancient custom: fishermen's families shaped garlands of flowers on frames of wood – one for each fishing boat. The garlands were paraded around the houses and then, after the blessing by the local vicar on the beach, each boat carried its garland out to sea and duly cast it overboard. The old folk said this May ritual was a legacy of pagan sea-god worship.

Mysteries are probably as irksome to some human minds as a grain of sand to an oyster. For others though mystery acts as a spur. Almost certainly curiosity prompted early man and woman to make their first journeys. 'What lies behind that hill?' The need to trade

Dorset has a haunted, haunting quality.

A time to contemplate the vista from Lyme Regis.

came later, and this Dorset atmosphere is especially powerful, beckoning us on and on.

Past happenings somehow generate an energy of their own: a ripple on the ether – as if these past happenings have imprinted themselves on the place and echoes are heard.

Dorset – or parts of it – undoubtedly have a haunted, haunting air.

Not surprising then that it is well populated with ghosts – that Peter Underwood, President of the Ghost Club, Britain's ghost hunter supreme, should have found it such rich fascinating territory. His *Ghosts of Dorset*, published by Bossiney in 1988, reveals a whole range of hauntings: a ghostly white donkey, a world-famous screaming skull, phantom coach-and-horses which Thomas Hardy used, a prehistoric 'Peeping Tom' and many more.

Moreover Dorset's haunted, haunting reputation lives on. As

A secret lane slips deep into a Dorset valley.

recently as February 1989, strange happenings occurred at The Bridport Arms Hotel at West Bay.

David Young came here for part of his TV series on haunted locations in the Westcountry. Normally the presence of TV cameras or radio recording equipment can be guaranteed to frighten off any ghosts. It seems as if the spirits are reluctant to be held on tape or film.

Was this though one exception to that reluctant pattern?

Journalist Margery Hull, writing in the *Bridport News* said: 'Ghostbuster Michael Williams has been called to investigate the strange manifestation . . . Mr Williams, a member of The Ghost Club, was alerted by Television South West's roving architect David Young

BRIDPORT ARMS HOTEL

when the features of a spooky spectre appeared on the ceiling of the pub's kitchen after television cameras had been filming.

'Said a puzzled Mr Williams: "I have been investigating supernatural happenings for almost 25 years and this is the first time I have encountered anything like this. The cynic might say the image could have been caused by smoke or heat. But in that case why wasn't there a similar image where the other television light was? . . . there is no doubt that the image is there and is very definitely a face. Sightings of ghosts and the sound of footsteps are legion but this is a very rare occurrence.'

Maureen Hyams, covering the eerie happenings at The Bridport Arms for *The Western Gazette* recalled the genuinely haunted reputation of the building, parts of which date back to the seventeenth century: 'In recent years staff at the seaside thatched hotel have had gas taps mysteriously turn themselves on, glasses start to rattle in the bar, and heard footsteps going upstairs.'

Residents have seen a figure during the night. Landlady Carla James told the newspapers: 'One girl woke up and thought she saw the figure of a man standing at the bottom of her bed but he simply disappeared. It is all very strange.'

The curious fact is the man's face with long dark hair and beard on the kitchen ceiling matched the description of that fleeting figure in the bedroom.

Is he the ghost of someone who knew the inn and is unwilling to leave it forever?

Time may or may not produce the answer, but, on the strength of this strange drawing, The Bridport Arms is worthy of inclusion in any mysterious tour of Dorset.

From a 1989 mystery to ancient mystery requires only the relatively short journey to the village of Winterbourne Abbas. Although they stand by the fast busy road, linking Bridport and Dorchester, the Nine Stones, even in our twentieth century, generate a sense of mystery. These Nine Stones, reminding us of Dame Barbara Hepworth's sculpture, form one of Dorset's rare stone circles.

The Bridport Arms Hotel scene of a modern mystery – whose was the bearded face etched on the ceiling?

They date from the early period of the Bronze Age and could well be connected with water worship. The clue is that nearby is the source of Winterbourne stream, and it is conceivable that the earliest water worship in the county took place here. To the old folk water was 'magic'. It held the gift of life and, in contrast, people drowned in water. Men and women saw their first images reflected in water. Wherever they found it bubbling up from the earth they reckoned they had found a sacred place.

Tom Lethbridge, who was known as 'the Einstein of the Paranormal', believed hauntings were often connected with the electrical field of water. Undeniably hauntings frequently occur in damp locations, and Lethbridge maintained such fields act as a sort of 'tape recorder'. They 'tape' strong emotions.

Author Colin Wilson, a celebrated presentday explorer into the Occult however thinks Lethbridge 'was only partially correct. It is not the 'field' of water that is involved, but the electrical field of the earth.'

Either way, it is an area which intrigues – firing speculation – while the stone circle remains a puzzle. Truly we are in *Unknown Dorset.*

Grey recumbent tombs of the dead in desert places
Standing stones on the vacant wine-red moor,
Hills of sheep, and the homes of the silent vanished races
and winds, austere, and pure . . .

The author of *Treasure Island* wrote those words long ago. Robert Louis Stevenson may not have been thinking specifically of Dorset, but his cleansing winds still flow across the varied and mysterious landscapes of this lovely, contrasting countryside – and in an off-beat way Dorset is a sort of Treasure Island.

Both of us live in Cornwall and in making this Dorset journey we are, in fact, following in famous Cornish footsteps. Lady Clara Vyvyan, that great Cornish travel writer who walked down the Rhone

Michael Williams and television presenter David Young peer at the mysterious outline of a bearded man's face on the ceiling.

All at peace as two walkers soak up Lyme Regis' special atmosphere.

on foot, enjoyed an Arctic adventure, and visited places as different as Greece and Ireland, the Scilly Isles and the Grand Canyon, rated a week's walking in Dorset one of her most memorable excursions. She recalled 'I walked on into unknown country;' so may be we are correct with our title after all.

Here in Dorset she wrote '. . . I came to world's end little valleys shut away from confusion, noise and sorrow; and to bare heights where austerity seems to answer every question.' Incredibly fifty years on, we too picked up such echoes.

'Grey recumbent tombs of the dead.' The tiny old church at Fleet near Weymouth. Much of this church was swept away in a great storm in the nineteenth century. Nowadays it is hard to believe disaster touched this peaceful, secret corner of Dorset.

Responding to the mystery and the magic

Dorset has the knack of working on people. Jeremy Irons, the actor, spent an important slice of his early years at Sherborne School. Here he is recalling those school days in *The Western Daily Press* in 1984:

'. . . Dusk down by the station, laying pennies on the train track at the level crossing, then lying with ears pressed against the polished steel listening for the hiss of the approaching monster. And then, all in a rush it would be upon us, making the road rumble as it roared past, great sparks spewing out of its funnel, on its way up or down from London.

'And oh, how in those days we longed to be on it, and home. As the level crossing gates swung open, the mutilated penny was retrieved, stuffed with grubby hands into the still unfamiliar suit pocket and the little group of newly made friends scurried back their lamplit way to communal tea.

'Favourite places were established and colonised. The secret gully reached by turning off the road running north out of the town. Where to? Without a map I cannot say, so the secret is secure.

'Known only to boys on bikes who probably still test their skill, their nerves and their machines, hurling themselves over the roller coaster track, pitting life and limb against the hidden roots, sudden bends, and maniacs going the wrong way. "The Bumps" it was

Dorset has a knack of working on people.

Part of Sherborne School captured on camera earlier this century.

known as. Whether this was an allusion to the topography or to the physical damage inflicted I never thought to ask.'

Jeremy Irons, who starred in *The French Lieutenant's Woman* shot at Lyme Regis, has said of Sherborne: 'This beautiful place has remained forever part of me.' Dorset goes to work on the creative spirit – stirring imagination and never letting go.

Dorset life has been full of character and characters – a quality which sometimes reads like fiction rather than fact. Take the case of John Love, bookseller of Weymouth; when he died in the autumn of 1793, in his 41st year he weighed 26 stone! Through a combination of over eating and drinking he was obliged to have the waistline of breeches nearly up to his chin to prevent their falling off. He often enjoyed his food and drink in his nightgown – and was seldom seen in a coat. But John Love was no Dorset record holder. One Benjamin Bower, who lived near Wimborne, died in the year 1736: the result of

Bow-fronted cottages at Lyme Regis with all the grace and charm of a by-gone age.

drinking a gallon of cider in the incredible belief that it would cure his gout! Mr Bower weighed no less than 34 stone and a bit more.

Excess of another kind was the habit of notorious Judge Jeffreys at his Bloody Assizes. A heavy drinker and possessing a vicious temper, Jeffreys was infamous – not just for his death sentences. Typical was the case of an unfortunate 14 year-old boy William Wiseman, apprenticed to a barber in Weymouth. A declaration was displayed in the seaside town by men of the Duke of Monmouth. Some of the people however were without basic education and could not read. They asked young William to read the declaration to them. *This* was his crime and Jeffreys sentenced him to be whipped through every

The promenade at Lyme Regis.

market town in the county – more than twenty. The sentence was carried out in first Dorchester and then Weymouth, by which time the evil judge had departed – and the sentence was sensibly stopped.

Little wonder that Jeffreys was unable to walk from his Dorchester lodgings to the court without fear of attack. The news of the Judge's death must have touched a chord of irony here in Dorset. He died, aged only 41, in the Tower of London, petrified lest he fell into the hands of the 'rabble'.

There is in Dorset a magnificent sense of continuity.

Sherborne demonstrates that ongoing quality: the ruins of 'old' Sherborne Castle stand on the other side of the lake from Sherborne 'new' Castle.

History stalks the Dorset landscape and nowhere more sharply than here. In the Spring of 1988 fellow Bossiney author Heidi Best came for a feature in the now sadly extinct *Dorset Tatler.*

'Time has so little touched Sherborne Castle and its sweeping acres that it is not difficult to picture the scene described by the distinguished gentleman sitting opposite me. He laughs as he recalls playing fox and hounds in the underground tunnels with his sisters and brother, fishing for pike in the lake, playing soldiers during the years of the First World War when the castle was a military hospital, and riding his pony in the green and pleasant park. But for the modern cars parked outside, there is little in view to indicate that over half a century has passed since those carefree days.

'Simon Wingfield Digby is terribly proud of Sherborne Castle. It has been his family's home since 1617 when it was given by James I to Sir John Digby (later created Earl of Bristol) as a reward after he had been given the unenviable task of trying to arrange the marriage between Charles, Prince of Wales and the Spanish Infanta. Nine years before, Sir Walter Raleigh and his family had lost possession of the Sherborne lease when the great Elizabethan seaman was forced to relinquish his leasehold to the Crown after being thrown into the

Sherborne Castle.

Fossil-laden cliffs back the town of Lyme Regis.

Tower of London on a charge of high treason. An error or omission in his will was to deprive his elder son, Wat, from customary inheritance. A sad day, indeed for Raleigh and his family, but it is, as they say, an ill wind . . .'

It is this intermingling of time which makes Dorset such a fascinating region. In the older corners you begin to feel past, present and future are all interlocked. Moreover it's not simply the richness of Dorset history or the fact the county is a mine of folklore. The essential magic of Dorset is in its atmosphere, and that quality is elusive, difficult to pin to paper like trying to build a cottage or a castle on reflections. The spirit cannot be captured – yet it is everywhere.

Lyme Regis cannot be part of *Unknown Dorset.* As a resort it is too well loved and well known.

Yet there is an element of mystery – mystery of deep and baffling nature. What triggers creativity is a curious something defying neat easy classification. It is this kind of mystery which hangs over Lyme Regis.

Jane Austen loved the place and made the Cobb famous as the location where Louisa Musgrove fell in *Persuasion* and, more recently, John Fowles used Lyme Regis as the setting for his classic *The French Lieutenant's Woman.*

No literary person can come to Lyme Regis and not think of Jane Austen. It remains a town of character, Georgian houses, tall cliffs of limestone. The harbour, caught in between the Cobb, that lovely curved wall to the west, and the jetty to the east, it is not surprising Miss Austen loved the place so. She holidayed here with her parents in the early 1800s, swimming every day, dancing at the local Assembly, and visiting a certain Mrs Armstrong 'who sat darning a pair of stockings the whole of my visit ...'

Lyme works on people. The great Tennyson came here, and, on arrival, refused all refreshment, insisting at once: 'Now take me to the Cobb and show me the steps from which Louise Musgrove fell.' It is that kind of place – where tradition and traditions are alive, ongoing, where spirits can be refreshed.

The Cobb at Lyme Regis from which Louisa Musgrove slipped in Jane Austen's Persuasion.

WILLIAM BARNES

Can it be sheer coincidence? Or is there something in the atmosphere which fires creativity? Indeed those questions pose themselves in Dorset as a whole.

Thomas Hardy remains forever a part of Dorset.

Thomas Hardy at his desk at Max Gate and Lawrence of Arabia in his austere cottage at Wool. There *has* to be a creative spirit here.

We must not forget William Barnes either. Overshadowed by the great gifted Hardy, many nevertheless regard Barnes as the finest poet to have written in English dialect. A Dorset man, he lived his whole life in the countryside, writing some of the most beautiful verses in the language, mostly in that delightful slow talk of the county. The son of a farmer, he was born in the Blackmore Vale and became a man of many roles: schoolmaster, solicitor's clerk, engraver and wood-cut artist. He was a master of language. In his high noon,

Poet William Barnes is immortalised on a statue in Dorchester.

he was capable of handling 60 languages, including Manchu, Egyptian and Chinese. He composed music, played four instruments and wrote books on subjects as diverse as economics and archaeology. Significantly too he influenced the early development of Hardy's literary genius. In his middle years he was ordained and eventually made Rector of Winterbourne Came near Dorchester where he gave almost a quarter of a century of devoted service to his parish and his people. Truly a multi-talented son of the Blackmore Vale – and a vivid reminder of Dorset's creativity.

In looking at the creativity of the county, we must not forget Dorset's distinguished painter James Thornhill. How many visitors to places like Blenheim Palace and Hampton Court, Chatsworth and Burghley House know the link with Dorset? The fact is many of his works grace rooms in those properties? You will find Thornhill portraits in establishments as diverse as All Souls, Oxford and the National Portrait Gallery, Trinity College, Cambridge and the Tate Gallery. Happily though examples of his work remain 'at home' in Dorset. You can see an altarpiece of his in St Mary's Church, Weymouth. You can also see a portrait of Sir James in the Guildhall; his portrait is near that of Sir Christopher Wren whom he succeeded as MP for Weymouth – curious to think that the two are linked in Dorset and St Paul's, London, where Thornhill decorated the interior of that magnificent dome. Curious too to reflect that though he was rated 'the greatest history painter this country has produced,' details of his early life remain obscure. We know he was born at Melcombe Regis, north of Weymouth, and that he learnt the rudiments of his art from another man of Dorset, Thomas Highmore.

So we further speculate on Dorset's ability to generate creativity.

Maybe there is no precise, concise answer. But there is something here, some space or some quality – room for our eternal quest for the unknown.

Dorset has a mysterious way of generating creativity. Quite what is that quality is difficult to determine but there is something here, some space or some quality – room for our eternal quest for the unknown.

Some Dorset surprises

Dorset has the ability to spring surprises.

Hitler, surely the most evil man in all history, who would link him with this most English of counties?

There is, in fact, a curious association, and you will find it in the original Keep of the Dorset's Depot on the western edge of Dorchester. This is the Dorset Military Museum which houses uniforms, medals, pictures – and a great deal more reflecting 250 years of fascinating military history.

Pride of place goes to a rather plain piece of furniture – Hitler's writing table. On it there is a letter from the Head Commissioner's office, Dusseldorf which reads: 'In September 1945 the Russian Army started to remove the furniture from Hitler's Chancellory in the Russian section in Berlin. The Russian Officer responsible for this work offered me a wooden writing table which he had taken from the head office. Those who visited the Chancellory in those days will remember that the whole place was in a state of great confusion with a large amount of furniture, some of it badly damaged, scattered in all directions.'

The Russian officer actually delivered the table to W H S Bishop, and he handed it over to his old regiment the Dorsetshire for their

Dorset Military Museum at Dorchester.

Dorset Military Museum

Author Michael Williams tries out Hitler's writing table.

museum. The letter is signed W H A Bishop, Major General (Retd) Commander, Northern Rhine, Wesphale, 22 March 1950.

The strange thing was that when Alison and I visited the museum neither of us experienced any unpleasant vibrations from the desk which makes us wonder whether the passage of time has somehow washed away the evil echoes.

From Hitler to cricket is a strange switch of direction. Yet again Dorset shows it has the ability to spring surprises.

How many cricket enthusiasts, for example, know of Gilbert Jessop's link with Dorset. Jessop, a cricketing legend for Gloucestershire, was the fastest-scoring batsman in the history of the game. In his career for Gloucestershire, Cambridge University and England he scored at the incredible rate of 79 runs an hour. They called him – 'The Croucher', a nick-name which derived from his stance at the crease. It also matched his fielding; in the covers his movements were positively electric. He stopped the ball and returned it with such speed and accuracy that it made Gilbert Laird Jessop one of the greatest fielders of all time.

In 1936 Mr Jessop and his wife came to live at their son's vicarage at St George's, Fordington, Dorchester. The Rev G L O Jessop, previously chaplain at Queen's College, Cambridge devoted himself to looking after his parents until their deaths some twenty years later.

It's a pretty safe bet though that the vast majority of cricket lovers who come to Dorset have no idea that Gilbert Jessop spent his evening years here far away from Gloucestershire. 'No man has ever driven a cricket ball so hard, so high, and so often in so many different directions. No man has ever made cricket so dramatic an entertainment.'

That was the verdict of C B Fry. Indeed Jessop lives on in the history and folklore of cricket, and Dorset should be proud of its association.

Another little known cricketing link with Dorset comes in the person of that much loved cricket commentator Brian Johnston. He spent a couple of boyhood years here, and still vividly remembers he and his brother being taken by their tutor to Bournemouth to see their first county cricket. Even at that early stage, his interest in the off-beat was already there, for all these years on, Brian Johnston recalls the considerable presence of Lord Lionel Tennyson fielding at mid-off – and the fact that Livsey, the wicket-keeper that day, was Tennyson's butler!

Adolf Hitler on a postage stamp.

Cricketing legend Gilbert Jessop who was the fastest scoring batsman in the history of the game.

Finally, to complete a cricketing hat-trick for Dorset, we find a connection with the first tour by English cricketers which should have taken place in Paris in 1789. A key figure in the organisation was the Duke of Dorset, Britain's Ambassador in Paris. The touring party duly travelled to Dover and were about to board the Channel ferry when they were met by the Duke of Dorset, fleeing from the French Revolution.

So the clash between sport and politics is clearly no modern problem.

Names can and do cause confusion. Rare is the individual who has not received a letter intended for somebody else. When a servant brought Dr Johnson a note, Johnson turned to his friend Boswell and said: 'An odd thought strikes me; we shall receive no letters in the grave.' That may or may not be so, but there is an element of confusion in Dorset sometimes over one name.

As Hardy overshadows Parson Barnes in the landscape of Dorset literature, so he overshadows or, at least, causes some confusion over the other Hardy: Nelson's Hardy. But there is no mistaking the Vice-Admiral's memorial tower high on Blackdown. Eighty feet high it has peerless views of the Dorset countryside and the English Channel.

We know the bare biographical bones but, in some important respects, Hardy remains a shadowy figure. Thomas Masterman Hardy came from an old Dorset family. He was born in 1760 at Kingston Russell, close to the village Long Bredy on the Burton Bradstock Road. His mother, a Russell, married Joseph Hardy of Portesham, an attractive village set in a valley at the foot of Blackdown. The sea is not far away and even then must have exerted an influence over the boy. The Hardys lived at a little Georgian Manor House fronting the village green. After a spell at the Old Grammar School at Milton Abbas, which was pulled down by Lord Milton to improve the view from his home, Hardy was sent off to sea at the age of twelve. After a year before the mast he was returned to school, but clearly had the sea in his blood because after three years at Crewkerne Grammar he ran away and joined the Merchant Marine as an ordinary seaman.

Later he joined the Royal Navy where his seamanship won him rapid promotion: a Lieutenant at the age of 21. It is the unknown element – that curious chemistry which brought Nelson and Hardy so close which intrigues. Initially it could be that Nelson saw Hardy merely as an outstanding young officer. Duty, loyalty and friendship

The childhood home of Thomas Masterman Hardy at Portesham.

read like cliches rather than explanations.

Maybe mutual debt came into the reckoning ultimately, for they saved one another's lives. That area of the relationship began in 1796: action between Nelson's two tiny frigates and a Spanish squadron. For the *only* time in his life Nelson was in danger of defeat and capture. Hardy, appreciating the danger, hoisted the English flag above the colours of his prize, drew the attentions of the Spaniards and enabled Nelson to escape. Hardy put up a brave fight but was captured. He was lucky however: exchanged for a Spanish prisoner, he rejoined Nelson.

Then came another incredible episode: off Gibraltar Nelson, with only one ship, was hotly pursued by a Spanish fleet. An English sailor fell overboard and Hardy, in a moment of madness or sheer heroism, jumped into a boat and put off to save the sailor. The Spaniards were

Bossiney artist Felicity Young's drawing of Vice-Admiral Hardy.

coming up fast, but Nelson had no hesitation and shouted: 'By God I'll not lose Hardy. Back the mizzen topsail!' The Spaniards, taken aback by the audacity, abandoned pursuit.

From the Battle of the Nile Hardy was Nelson's flag captain. Hardy was with him at the Battle of Copenhagen and in the long patient waiting and watching for Villeneuve. He was ready too when Nelson came aboard *Victory* for his last battle. Although Nelson rated his band of brothers highly, Hardy undoubtedly had a special place – he was witness of Nelson's last will, and they were together when Nelson made the crucial decision to break the enemy line at Trafalgar.

They stood together in that moment of triumph and tragedy on *Victory* when Nelson was hit by a sniper's bullet. 'They have done for me at last!' said the admiral as they carried him below, but Nelson covered his face and medals so that his men should not see that he had been hit. The battle raged on and Hardy, now in command of the fleet, stayed on deck, but Nelson kept calling for him:

'How goes the battle, Hardy?'

'Anchor, Hardy, anchor!' the realisation that a tempest was to come.

Then the pathetic cry: 'Don't throw me overboard, Hardy.'

At the end: 'Kiss me, Hardy.' The dying admiral opened his eyes: 'Who is that!' 'It is Hardy' came the reply. 'God bless you, Hardy.' Those were Nelson's last words. But there is another version: some say Nelson merely said 'Kismet, Hardy' Cruel Fate it certainly was.

Thereafter there were no more battles for Thomas Masterman Hardy. Instead 30 years of distinguished service: Baronet, Vice-Admiral, Commander in home and American waters.

After Trafalgar, Hardy decided it was time to marry. Louisa Hardy was flighty. She had been a Berkeley and consequently considered herself far above the plain old Hardys. Her life was largely a dizzy round of society gatherings. The marriage could not have been that close because flirtatious Louisa's husband was often away, sometimes for several years at a stretch.

Hardy's last appointment was as Governor of Greenwich Hospital where he died in 1839. He is buried in the mausoleum there. Later Louisa married her patient lover Lord Seaford. Though something of an enigma Hardy lives on in the folklore of the sea.

Here in Dorset he is remembered with pride, and, on a good day, his tower commands views of the Channel from Start Point in Devon to the Isle of Wight.

A magnificent pair of horses at Dorset Heavy Horse Centre.

Time shapes curiosity. Today's most modern motor car will one day end up in a museum. Our most sophisticated computers will, at some point, become antiques. If we look at old prints and photographs, we will see that the horse once dominated the Dorset countryside.

Today though he is relatively rare. The tractor, the car, the bus and the lorry have all replaced him on our roads. So, in a significant way, the horse is part of past or unknown Dorset. A visit therefore to the Dorset Heavy Horse Centre is not only a delight for animal lovers, but curiously a kind of step back in time.

Poet and playwright, farmer and horseman, Ronald Duncan thoughtfully wrote:

The Horse

Where in this wide world can
man find nobility without pride,
friendship without envy or beauty
without vanity? Here, where
grace is laced with muscle, and
strength by gentleness confined.

He serves without servility; he has
fought without enmity. There is
nothing so powerful, nothing less
violent, there is nothing so quick,
nothing more patient.

England's past has been borne on
his back. All our history is his
industry; we are his heirs, he
our inheritance.

Enjoying the pasture at Dorset Heavy Horse Centre.

The harness room.

Set in lovely countryside on the edge of the New Forest, the Dorset Heavy Horse Centre offers us the unique opportunity of seeing some of the finest Shire, Clydesdale, Ardennes, Percheron, Suffolk Punch and Canadian-Belgian heavy horses in the country.

Time was in Britain when these gentle giants of the horse kingdom were the backbone of British agriculture, but progress, in

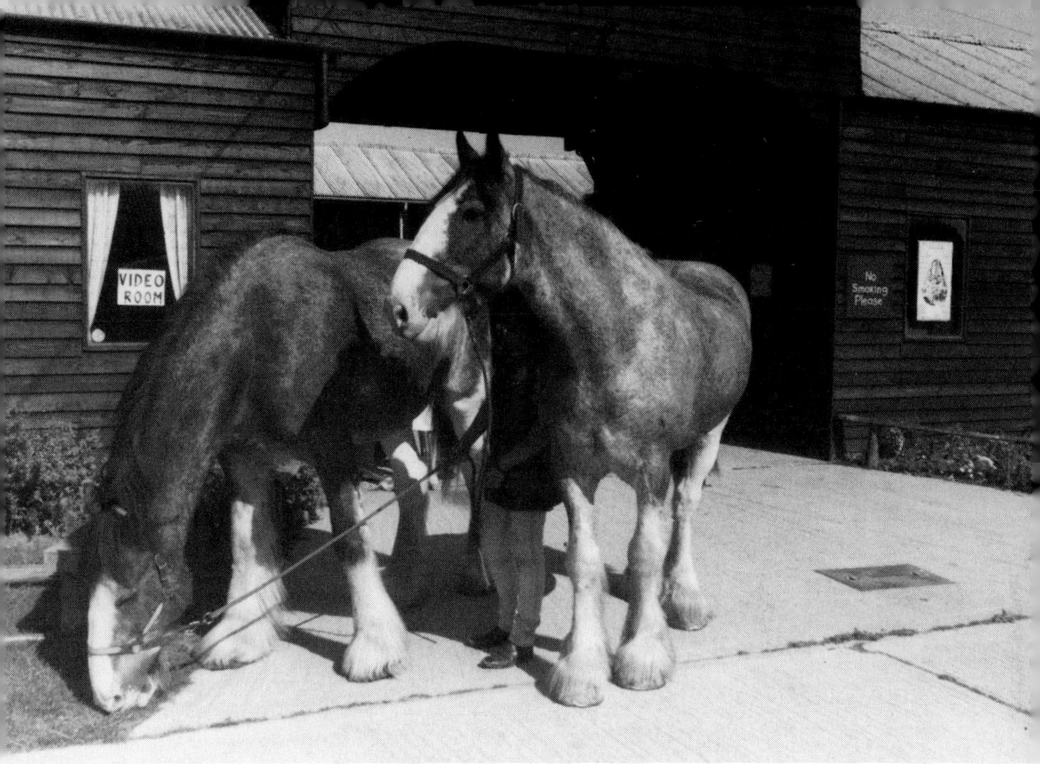

A fine pair of horses.

the shape of mechanisation, resulted in their decline. However curiously, fortunately the popularity of the big horse is returning; you have only to go to our county shows or see how they are being used in the modern publicity and promotion.

The commendable aim of the centre here at Verwood is to preserve our rich agricultural heritage by providing a showplace for these magnificent horses who were once an everyday sight in the countryside of Dorset.

The admirable Dorset Heavy Horse Centre brochure also gives an interesting insight into history:

'Practically all Heavy Horses in the world today are descended from original 'Flanders' horses. 'Flanders' horses were the original war-horses – as used by William the Conqueror at the Battle of Hastings in 1066. The rider, his armour, and the horse-armour weighed a total of about 7 cwt. Interesting to note that William won the battle because his soldiers were mounted. Had they not been, would he have won, and how might our country's history be different?

Before we go any deeper into *Unknown Dorset,* we should perhaps try to justify such a title. We believe definition is often a matter of interpretation. Recently in the course of researching something quite different, we came across an early and long out of print Bossiney title *Facets of Crime.*

In it Ronald Duncan wrote: 'The reason why I am interested in crime is because I am a criminal. It is true that I have not been arrested, commited or sentenced – for any major offence. But like Goethe, I am aware that "there is no crime which I have not contemplated committing."

'What distinguishes a man of untarnished reputation from a crook? The difference lies not in their natures or inclinations, but rather in the circumstances which surround them, their so-called "social environment", or in the degree of internal or external pressure which accompanies their impulse to act in what society calls an immoral or criminal way. But any man with any self-knowledge has to admit that the difference between himself and any criminal is too slight for him to be complacent or self-righteous. Possibly the main difference between the two is that the criminal enacts where other men merely indulge in fantasies which are sufficient to sublimate or satisfy them. In other words, the criminal lacking sufficient imagination for his mind to encompass and sustain him is driven into action to fulfil the dream which his mind cannot complete and thus he sleep-walks into crime, as it were, caught in his nightshirt. Whereas those of us who can daydream and fill our fantasies with sufficient detail keep the right side of the law. Indeed, we become the law itself.'

Hopefully then we may have confused your definition or prejudice about the word *unknown.*

Even behind the elegant and the seemingly obvious can lie rare quality. How many visitors in the rolling landscape of West Dorset know the full significance of Parnham, a beautiful house with gardens to match, just one mile south of Beaminster?

Parnham is more than a magnificently restored Tudor manor house. Its unique spirit inspired John Makepeace, the designer and maker of fine furniture, to establish his family home, his furniture businss and the international School for Craftsmen in Wood here. Wherever you go in Parnham House, you will be touched by the superb craftsmanship in wood. Try and plan your visit here for a Wednesday from April till October when you are invited to see the

Parnham House, Beaminster. On medieval foundations, this Tudor Manor was enlarged by John Nash in 1810. It has decorative ceilings and stained glass in mullioned windows. Parnham is the home of John Makepeace, the furniture designer and maker, and of the School for Craftsmen in Wood.

craftsmen at work. This is a place to both surprise and calm our senses: the beauty of the old trees, the sweeping green lawns, the wildlife of the River Brit – all to soothe – and then the surprises around every corner: the sculpture and the fountains. Not for long will Parnham qualify for inclusion in *Unknown Dorset,* for under Jennie Makepeace's imaginative supervision the gardens are becoming more and more famous.

Just four miles away, Parnham is establishing its new college at

A chair of superb quality in English Holly. Designed by John Makepeace and made in his workshops at Parnham by Alan Amey.

Hooke Park. Not only have the exciting new buildings attracted interest, but the concept is internationally relevant. The purpose is to develop and teach those technologies which will enable indigenous woodlands to become re-integrated with sustainable local industries, the produce being turned into high quality buildings, furniture and domestic products. Hooke Park College is pioneering this work and it opened to students at Easter 1989. Visitors to the woodland are welcome on Wednesday and Sunday afternoons (April to October), 2pm – 5pm.

All of which brings us again back to the creative spirit of Dorset. Cornwall is another creative area, and the Cornish painter Margo Maeckleberghe once when asked about atmosphere – the spirit which fires creativity – replied: 'The most important part for me is this mysterious X an artist *must feel* about a place to paint it.'.

Maybe that indefinable something makes Dorset such an exciting place too.

But before you leave Parnham House, where the Strodes lived for three centuries, spare a thought for young Lieutenant Rhodes-Moorhouse VC. He was one of the men of Beaminster who went to fight for King and Country in the 1914-18 war. On a bombing raid, he was shot up while flying low over German lines. He returned the 35 miles to land his plane back at headquarters, but died later that day. His body was sent home and he is buried here on the hill overlooking his old home, with his son who died in the Battle of Britan.

At Poole we found an interesting Cornish connection. Poole, like the Lizard, the most southerly part of Britain, which is the heel of Cornwall, is a cradle of wireless. Although not the first wireless station in the world, here in a small sitting room, only eighteen feet square, the great Marconi carried out many of his earliest experiments. A wireless station had been established on the Needles in 1896, and twelve months later another station was established in a basement close to the pier approach at Bournemouth. It proved unsuitable and Marconi with his assistant G S Kemp moved their pioneering apparatus to The Haven Hotel at Parkstone, part of Poole, and this modest room was to play a major role in linking the world by wireless. These experiments in Dorset directly led to the creation of the Poldhu Station at the Lizard.

We wondered if Lady Vyvyan, that distinguished Lizard resident,

The Haven Hotel, Parkstone, Poole, where the great Marconi carried out many of his earliest experiments with wireless.

knew of this fascinating Dorset-Cornwall communications history.

More than once on this journey we thought of Lady Clare Vyvyan, and at one point discussed making notes on the spot. Curiously enough the Cornish traveller had once talked about this very point.

'How do you write . . . from notes or from memory?' had been the question.

'Both,' came her reply. 'Thankfully I've been blessed with a good memory, though descriptive notes made en route have helped me, I wish I had made more of them. But often the really penetrating vision comes afterwards. There's something piercing at the time, yes, but later on, much later on, the whole thing stands out more clearly.'

Of her writing technique she explained: 'I go inch by inch. Variety in the size of the paragraphs is a good thing, the different lengths help the reader and for this reason, I don't think you can properly assess your work until you read it in type-written form.'

We have not attempted to do 'a Lady Vyvyan' in terms of travel

Marconi is remembered at The Haven Hotel with a lounge named after him.

writing, preferring to rely on the illustrations letting them tell their story. Ray Bishop, our most prolific Bossiney photographer, was seeing and photographing Dorset for the first time for many years. He relished the variety and particularly the subtle changes in mood and light, the contrast of land and seascape.

For the rest of this journey across *Unknown Dorset,* your travelling companion will be Alison Poole.

You could not have better company. For all her Bristol background and the fact that she lives and works in Cornwall, Alison has a great affinity with Dorset – something deeper than family links.

She not only cares for Dorset, loves the place in fact, but she understands its shade and subtlety. Whether one is thinking in words or visually in terms of pictures, you cannot say Dorset is instantly this or that. You cannot describe it in a word or visualise it in a second. There is simply no simple single clear-cut image.

Alison Poole understands all this – Dorset's essential magic.

About the author
ALISON POOLE

Alison Poole is a Bristolian with her heart firmly rooted in the Westcountry. Educated at Wycliffe School for Girls, Clevedon, she lives with her husband, a surveyor, their two daughters, and a cat on Bodmin Moor. A well-known Westcountry journalist, she has lived in Cornwall since 1977.

A Scorpio subject, she is interested in history, archaeology – and tap dancing. In the autumn of 1988 Alison became Bossiney editor, and earlier this year contributed a highly acclaimed chapter entitled Harvest of Mystery in 'Wiltshire Mysteries': an investigation into the phenomenon of strange circles in Wiltshire cornfields.

Here as co-author, Alison Poole explores one of her favourite regions. 'As a child Dorset was synonymous with summer', she said. 'There was so much family history there and the Days Out when we headed for Weymouth, Burton Bradstock or Lulworth were always special. I don't ever remember it raining at all. In fact it was at Weymouth that my parents joined a post-war queue to buy a wedding ring which father later produced with a flourish on the beach. Sadly the magic moment of proposal was marred by two beastly little boys who popped up from behind a rock smirking.'

Alison Poole

Secret past

DORSET is an enigma. Softly rounded, she spreads her curves across the land. Not for Dorset the jagged edges or discordant bumps of suburbia.

Like an elusive lover she welcomes the centuries but never wholly surrenders. No matter how hard the ages try to leave a lasting stamp on the countryside, the age-old quality fights back seeming to say: 'Don't come too close'. It holds the secret of what has passed and perhaps what is yet to come.

Clouds are so much a part of Dorset; they build and shred before the wind but they are always there. The land is brushed with a blue-green sheen of fecundity. And while electricity pylons stride across the landscape Dorset looks to her enduring prehistoric traces, 'It will pass', she says with a shrug.

The past is all around. Sometimes it feels omnipresent. It seems that wherever one looks there is a hill fort, encampment, barrow or standing stone. It must have been heavily populated thousands of years ago.

Perhaps one of the most intriguing and secret little places is a tiny stone circle at Winterbourne Abbas, the Nine Stones. It lies right beside the main road from Bridport to Dorchester just before the village with only a row of plain black railings to keep the trucks at bay.

Enter the little gate and it is another time and place. There is a remarkable sense of peace. Michael Williams, photographer Ray Bishop and I visited it one warm spring morning when the rooks were

A tucked away corner of Dorset.

The Nine Stones at Winterbourne Abbas.

busy building their nests high in the trees. Bluebells tinted the woods behind the stones and the scent of wild garlic floated on the air.

The Department of the Environment metal noticeboard boldly states that it is a 'small stone circle 25 feet in diameter, constructed in the Bronze Age and used for religious purposes'. I wish I had their confidence. Whatever the stones were used for it felt as though it must have been good; there is a kind of quiet reverence there under the tall trees with the sunlight filtering through. One of the stones has been embraced by the knobbly roots of a huge tree.

Not far from The Nine Stones, in folding land behind Askerswell, is Eggardon Hill. Some 800 feet above the shining sea to the south this 20 acre Iron Age hill fort, with its triple banks and ditches, is a lasting monument to those Dorset men of long ago who built it. A fully-grown stag skipped across the road when I made my pilgrimage to this breezy hillside. He hopped over the fence

Rooks nest high in the trees.

effortlessly and cantered away into the archaeological distance.

Prehistoric hillforts proliferate. Further to the west of Eggardon Hill is Pilsdon Pen. At 909 feet it is the highest hill in Dorset and crowned by more ancient earthworks. Then away to the east are Badbury Rings, another fort and now in the caring hands of the National Trust. Years ago these wonderful banks and ditches, dressed with hawthorn and brambles, were much abused. But now the trust has done much to restore them, if not to their former state – which would have been a crowded town – certainly to a more ecologically sound footing.

Seatown

DORSET'S coast is unique. A friend of mine has a theory that she could be blindfolded and left anywhere in England and would quickly work out roughly what county she was in because of the soil's colour, the architecture and building materials. Certainly there could be no doubt of location if dumped on the grating, golden pebbles of Chesil.

Chesil Beach, running 20 miles from Bridport to Portland Bill is one of Nature's wonders. This massive pebble bank rims the coast and keeps the sea firmly away from the delicate sandy cliffs.

Even in winter, when winds howl off the Channel and Chesil's great heaving mass groans at the buffeting of a sea that foams in anger, summer images linger. There are the windbreaks strung out in coloured splashes away from the security of the refreshment kiosks. And darting between sea and 'camp' – provided by towels, rugs, thermos flasks, sandwiches and books – are the brave English-white bodies determined to get a reddish tinge, if not a tan.

Seatown, just a couple of miles off the main coast road at Chideock is a classic. It personifies the small beach resorts that cling to the foot of Dorset's cliffs along the Chesil. There are charming cottages, houses and an unobtrusive caravan site.

Golden Cap in all its 600 foot glory peers down from the west while on the other side of this geological gash – caused no doubt, if geography teachers are to be believed, by a much larger version of the harmless stream that sneaks through the valley – are colours. Green, burnished sandstone and old gold, streaked through with brown, are exposed by the weather-cut cliff face. The shingle of the beach seems

'Dorset's coast is unique.'

almost pink in comparison, stretching the length of Chesil right out to hazy Portland.

A swim on this stretch of coast is not for the faint-hearted. Even on a quiet day it needs care. Father used to encourage me to screw up courage and get in as he trod water in the relative calm of ten yards offshore. There was a trick, he said, you had to time the waves just right, rather like running through a skipping rope. Once in you had to swim quickly out of the undertow's grasp.

Fine, but then getting out was another matter. The times I have been lifted by a huge wave and deposited unceremoniously with grazed knees on the painful, pebbly edge. The indignity didn't stop there. It was a desperate struggle to escape, usually on all fours, before another massive punch of green water dictated the future.

'Hazy Portland.'

A little pub, so beloved of summer visitors, sits at the foot of the valley looking firmly out to sea. And on a piece of green in front of it lies a chunk of folk history – a large rusting anchor.

The anchor was caught by West Bay fisherman Jack Woolmington when he was trawling 70 yards from the beach between Moonfleet, towards Portland, and Lyme Regis. Little did Jack know, when he fished it out, the tale that lay behind the anchor.

The huge rusting anchor at Seatown.

The Hope of Amsterdam, a 350 ton, 30 gun ship with a cargo of £50,000 of gold and silver, was on its way from Curacao to Amsterdam in the eighteenth century when it struck Chesil. The crew, apparently, managed to scramble to safety, but heavy seas broke the ship into three. The top deck was thrown on to the beach, the cabin was buried and the hull dragged out to sea and never found.

By the following day 2,000 villagers were ready for a bit of pillaging. And within a week there were more than 10,000 people from West Dorset, organised into parties of 20, digging for treasure.

One unfortunate character didn't get away with his enterprise. Augustin Elliott was tried at Dorchester in 1749 with 'feloniously carrying away part of the Hope's cargo, 10oz of gold and 20oz of silver', says the board in front of the anchor. After a long trial Augustin was acquitted, which said much for the British sense of fair play. It was decided that in view of the large numbers on the beach after the shipwreck it was impossible to find a jury in Dorset that was not in some way involved!

Maiden Castle

NO history book had prepared me for Maiden Castle. As a child it was a tantalising glimpse as the family motor hot-footed for a day's outing on the rasping pebbles of Weymouth beach.

'That's Maiden Castle over there', Mother would say. 'Looks fascinating doesn't it?' But there was never time to stop and explore. The pull of a swim at Weymouth, a picnic lunch and a cup of tea from the Primus stove always proved too much.

It seems strange that it wasn't until I was the mother of an historically minded daughter myself that I actually crossed the threshold of this, the largest earthworks in England, and discovered one of Britain's most impressive relics.

It seemed more fitting to call at the castle's back door one sharp, grey morning in early Spring than march boldly up to the towering front entrance. The road through Winterbourne Monkton looks for all the world as though it is a private drive, but just a short distance from the village the edge of Maiden's ramparts are clearly visible on the right.

A short steep climb along a field's edge leads to the English Heritage black iron kissing gate and into another time.

With the sun streaking through the clouds, a Sparrow Hawk kept its lonely vigil high above the earthworks while all around was the song of larks. It was solitary and other-worldly that day as the first stirrings of spring began the age-old cycle of re-birth; a reminder of the continuity of the seasons which would have been followed so closely by the community in the fort.

Away to the south of this magnificent piece of prehistoric engineering the heavy lorries thunder along the main road on their

The author Alison Poole ponders on the immensity of Maiden Castle.

ceaseless task of supplying the needs of the twentieth century householder.

How different it would have been for the residents of this township perched high above sea level. No nipping down to Tesco for a few things to top up the larder but rather a self sufficient ideal for the community as a whole to best the weather and try to keep warm and fed.

Maiden Castle has a long history. It was first settled some 2,000 years before Caesar's forces landed. The original fort enclosed just ten acres and is thought to have been used solely as a safe place to sleep at night. Then this arrangement appears to have been abandoned. Nobody quite knows why, after several centuries, it was no longer used but certainly it fell into disuse. Some time later a

Maiden's ramparts stretch into the distance.

massive burial mound, 1,790 feet in length, was built for one very important man.

Whoever this VIP was, his skull had been pierced and his arms and legs broken, perhaps as part of some magical rite.

Maiden Castle seems to have been re-populated in the early part of the Iron Age. A new wall was built, this time enclosing sixteen acres with eastern and western entrances. It was soon found that these entrances were a weak link in the fort's security and were beefed up with new stone-faced walls.

After a few centuries suddenly, and for no apparent reason, the fort was expanded to incorporate a massive 45 acres instead of 16. Certainly a case of urban regeneration or perhaps a population explosion.

Back in the '30s Sir Mortimer Wheeler, the renowned archaeologist, carried out a massive and systematic dig. In his book *Maiden Castle, Dorset,* he says that the high and involved defences had long been recognised as the most imposing of their class.

After the fort had been increased to 45 acres: 'The earthwork remained in the occupation of a considerable if squalid urban peasantry until the middle of the first century BC', says Sir Mortimer.

More civil engineering went on around the end of the first century BC. Outer ramparts and ditches were added and the main rampart was doubled in height to increase the fort's defence systems.

But although life went on for a while, and even coinage was introduced in the town, an efficient enemy was on the horizon. 'In or shortly after AD432 the Roman army of conquest, led by the future emperor Vespasian stormed the fortifications and a war cemetery within the outworks of the eastern entrance is a vivid memorial of the event.'

The subjugated citizens of Maiden – those who survived – had to

A visitor to Maiden Castle rests after his climb.

The outline of a Roman Temple.

stay on in their hilltop home while the Romanisation of the surrounding countryside went on apace.

The castle's inhabitants gradually drifted away and centuries later, when Rome's sun was setting, a small Roman temple was built among the ruins of the derelict township – maybe for a Roman purist who didn't hold with the Christian faith and wanted to get away from it all.

The past was underfoot as I clumped across the broad flat sward where once generations of Britons lived out their lives within the ramparts protective arms. Dorchester was away to the right in a tidy huddle of red brick with a Monday aura of domesticity wrapped around it.

But there was nothing comfortable about the sensation as I walked to the edge of a rampart to get a better look. The sheer drop into one of the fort's ditches was frightening. It was like looking out of a 'plane window with Lilliputian countryside spread out below and that awful tingling in the toes as though the little bit of support between stability and fresh air was about to evaporate. How on earth those men built such an enormous defence against the neighbours before the days of JCBs – and in all probability on low protein diets too – is a mystery.

Slithering down a bank as high as a house with frost particles just beginning to yield to the pale sun's caress, there was another shock in store. That wasn't the edge back there. Another sheer drop to the plain below confirmed the belief that attackers would have had little chance of success from this side of the castle.

A lone barrow away in the distance punctuated the flat land below, while far away the tangle of radio masts at an RAF station showed that defence was still on the minds of the chiefs.

A display board put up by English Heritage says that there is evidence of roads, houses with hearths and artisans such as weavers, carpenters, toolmakers and jewellers would have plied their trade in what was once a busy, crowded town.

Standing there, perhaps in someone's living room, it was hard to believe just how vast that fortified hilltop is. Just a short step in the imagination and there were the hundreds, if not thousands, of people bustling about their business. Would they have differed from us all that much? Certainly they must have lived and loved, laughed and cried while the very business of life in all its humdrum regularity plodded on. Warmth and cold, food and hunger, death and birth, while the petty jealousies and ambitions must surely have flourished amid it all.

On that bright, stinging morning, when even the faithful walkers of dogs were still engaged elsewhere, that town came to life. I didn't see anonymous bumps and dips in an expanse of sheep grazed turf; no, *they* were there with the woodsmoke from their fires shredding before the speeding wind. A smell of cooking. But no council men to take away the unwanted smells of decaying rubbish and no water authority to attend to the sanitation of a community.

Squalor would have stalked the scene of a prehistoric town without the modern injection of Third World aid. But a town that was vibrantly alive nevertheless.

A touch of magic

THE bumpy, narrow road to Arne leads to a magical land.

The Arne peninsula in its heath colours of pinks and golds, browns and greens, spreads out ahead and shows that here is a haven of peace for wildlife, and man too, if he respects it.

This charming chunk of land pokes out into Poole Harbour. It is one of the last remnants of heathland that once covered much of southern Britain and extends to Middlebere, Slepe and Stoborough Heath – a huge stretch of ancient land to the south east of Wareham.

The little switchback road heads straight for the village of Arne and a car park. On the way there are glimpses of the vast stretch of harbour etched as blue as the colour on Poole's famous pottery.

The Forestry Commission has planted a good deal of land with firs but where, in other parts of England, this is often lamented, here on this soil it enhances rather than detracts. The secret, pine scented woods hold a fragrant dark mystery.

The Royal Society for the Protection of Birds established a nature reserve here in 1965 and now it covers 1,200 acres of the peninsula. It is, as the RSPB says, 'A fine example of lowland heath' and has conserved a wildlife habitat that elsewhere is rapidly disappearing.

It really is an enthusiast's paradise. The three main types of heather: ling, cross-leaved heath and bell heather grow on the reserve and the less well-known Dorset heath is also found. More than 500 species of plants and insects thrive on this tract of land. The Dartford Warbler breeds on the heath as do many other birds such as meadow pipits, stonechats and the romantic nightjar. The small red damselfly, Downy Emerald dragonfly and a myriad butterflies dance across the vegetation, while all six British reptiles make Arne their home. The

Dorset's incomparable heathland.

seldom seen smooth snake and sand lizard dart about their business here too.

A public footpath from the car park at Arne village leads to Shipstal Point and a nature trail, a delight in itself. But for the more dedicated a permit from the RSPB warden is needed to enter the rest of the reserve.

The village of Arne, embraced by trees and birdsong, is small – it always has been. Even in the Domesday survey of 1086 it did not merit a separate mention and up until the sixteenth century it belonged to the Abbey of Shaftesbury. For the handful of tenants on this far-flung Dorset outpost it was a struggle to wrest a living from the poor soil but there were two other industries to help eke out.

From Roman times the villagers of Arne produced salt by boiling and evaporating sea water and then trading it for other goods; salt was even used as currency. Remains of the tough clay brick vessels called salterns have been found nearby and there is even a Salterns

Stretches of ancient heathland still exist in Dorset.

Copse. These clay vessels were replaced in medieval times by leaden containers called plumba, from the Latin plumbum meaning lead. Shaftesbury Abbey's twelfth century rent roll records that 20 tenants were employed in salt production and that a hide of land was devoted to the industry.

The sea yielded another crop for the residents of Arne – oysters. Even now the beach at Shipstal Point is often covered with oyster shells but in its heyday oysters dredged from these waters supplied London in a big way. Oysters used to be called the poor man's food but now, through over-fishing, pollution and disease, they are no longer plentiful, only pricey.

St Nicholas Church at Arne is special. It sits with a simple quiet dignity a few feet above the road looking out towards Poole Harbour. The name Arne comes from the Saxon 'Aerne' meaning secret place and that certainly is true.

This tiny thirteenth century church was built on the orders of an Abbess of Shaftesbury around 1220. It was originally a chantry but

St Nicholas Church, Arne.

later was annexed as a chapel of ease to the Church of Holy Trinity at Wareham.

The building is framed with trees. Inside the parishioners have polished and painted so that it is a well-kept delight. There are candle brackets on the walls, bench ends, and two large circular metal holders hang from the ceiling – but there is no sign of electric light at all. There is an overall theme of blue, purple and white inside, quite how I am unsure, it must be from curtains, hassocks and altar hangings but the overall impression is lovely. The altar itself has quite a history, it was made from a pre-Reformation stone with five small crosses carved on it which was found buried outside the church.

I fell in love with Arne one warm spring morning, it was so rich. Soft green moss grew in luxuriance, bluebells were forcing up through the warm, moist earth and the birds, of which there are so many, were singing fit to burst. How could I resist?

Studland Bay

ACROSS the narrow sea channel that twice daily fills and empties Poole Harbour, lies the grey hatched area of Bournemouth – a smart seaside town on a predictable pattern. But on the channel's right hand bank is Studland Bay, deserted, often desolate, and if not unknown, at least undeveloped.

This huge curving arc of sticky brown sugar-like sand covers miles of deserted beach backed by heathland. Its identity is entirely its own. The pleasure of up-market Bournemouth may be just across the bay while Swanage round the corner tempts the tourist too, but Studland stands firm, unwilling to compromise its heritage.

I re-visited it one wet, cold afternoon when rain was wrapping a fine clammy embrace around the place. It did not matter. If anything it was a better way to see Studland Bay with the sand dunes pitted with raindrops and water dripping from the eaves of neglected beach huts. Better times would come again.

Studland village is on top of the hill before the road dips down towards the heath and sea. Possibly this hill was steeper years ago because my mother remembers her father steadfastly refusing to drive down a hill marked as 'dangerous to cyclists'. That he was in a motor car made little difference, it was walk to the beach or don't go at all.

There is a toll booth further along where visitors pay to drive the last mile or so to the chain driven ferry which takes them to Sandbanks and the east coast. The huge bowl of Poole Harbour, dotted with islands, lies away to the north with Newton Heath, unspoilt and impenetrable, in the foreground.

Studland Bay has long attracted the hardy beach afficionado who

Studland Bay – space and safe swimming.

wants some space and safe swimming. The gaggle of ageing beach huts below the National Trust car park are testimony to that. It seems sad that the simple pleasure of two weeks good old fashioned bucket and spade holiday no longer holds such an attraction when weighed against the more sophisticated pleasures of overseas travel.

A beach hut was the ultimate in luxury back in the 50s. It was somewhere to brew up on a little camping stove, a place to change out of wet things after a shivering dip. And it was somewhere to cower while the rain drove in angry grey squalls against the walls to ooze through ill-fitting windows and form a puddle on the linoleum-covered floor. Optimism always remained high with the encouraging words 'Just a clearing shower', uttered with cheerful conviction.

As a boy my father spent many school summer holidays camping at Preston, near Weymouth. Grandfather used to pile the Morris Cowley with old ridge tent, camping gear, three boys and Gran and drive from Bristol to dump the lot of them for six weeks. He went

The vast expanse of sugar-like sand at Studland stretches towards Sandbanks on the other side of Poole Harbour.

down at weekends but only had one week's holiday a year himself so the family had a high old time of it while he worked.

At weekends a favourite place for a day out was Studland. 'In the 30s', said my father, 'there was virtually nothing there at all just a great big sandy area with sand dunes and bits of shell clinging to them.' It was a good place for swimming, though a little windy on occasions, and ideal for a bit of French cricket with the other intrepid families on the beach. Very often other lads joined the outing having met up at the camping field. It seemed a carefree, open armed existence until the 1939-45 war came along and blotted it out.

The war turned its sights on Studland in the autumn of 1940 when the beach was commandeered as an experimental anti-invasion site. By the summer of 1942 the heathland between Studland and Poole Harbour was being used as a battle range and soon after the roads to the ferry and Corfe Castle were closed to the public.

Studland echoed to the sound of the military rehearsing for its big

General Eisenhower was said to have watched battle rehearsals at Studland.

One of the pillboxes built at Studland during the 1939-45 war.

Fortifications from the 1939-45 war, so solid it seems they will last for ever.

scenario. Many villagers had to leave their homes as the activity intensified. Most of the north beach was used as a mock landing zone practising for the invasion of Europe and in fact several large trial battles were held there. On the cliffs some Canadian engineers built a 'massive observation post, heavily concreted and labelled on its rear wall – Fort Henry'. In fact Fort Henry, which took the name of a much earlier castle at Studland, played host to some VIPs including Winston Churchill, Eisenhower and Montgomery who watched the trials from the lookout's reinforced safety.

Before D day – June 5, 1944 – the whole of Christchurch, Poole and Swanage Bays were crammed with shipping while before dawn

Winston Churchill and General Montgomery who watched battle trials from Fort Henry at Studland.

hundreds of aircraft streamed off to France. The remarkable thing was that before daybreak the entire coast was empty.

After the war a massive cleaning up operation took place. The heath was systematically cleared of missiles and bombs. Over two years some 85,000 weapons were removed. But the odd pillbox here and there, so solid it seems they will endure for ever, still poke out from strategic points, as a forbidding reminder that Studland has not always been carefree.

Crowning glory

THE Earl of Antrim, has, what must surely be, the finest monument any man could wish for – the 619 foot high sandstone tipped Golden Cap, the highest cliff in the south of England.

The Earl was chairman of the National Trust from 1966 until his death in 1977 and the local stone memorial on the very top of Golden Cap bears the inscription: 'Given by members of the National Trust and friends in memory of the Earl of Antrim KBE . . .'

The trust owns now fewer than 1,974 acres of hill, cliff, farmland, undercliff and beach including some five miles of coast between Charmouth and Eypemouth which all adds up to the splendid Golden Cap Estate – a walker's paradise.

But the Cap itself is undoubtedly Dorset's crowning glory. It reigns supreme and commands respect by sheer dazzling colour and size. It can be seen from miles inland, up coast as far as Portland and even from the cliffs of Devon to the south west.

There are several ways to tackle its breath-taking heights. Perhaps the gentlest and most attractive is from Langdon Hill above the village of Chideock. The 48-acre wood of beech, Corsican and Scots pine is dark and still. Just the whisperings of small creatures and the occasional chafing and crack of a bough in the wind.

The track winds around the hill like a pale tan belt of clay.

Flat-topped Golden Cap, the highest cliff in the south of England.

Golden Cap on an old picture postcard with cows having a quiet paddle instead of holidaymakers.

Through the trees to the left is the valley leading to Seatown and the cliffs beyond.

The fragrant bluey-green pines frame the pale turquoise of the sea, and on a warm afternoon, with sun flashing through the trees, it seems almost mediterranean.

Away to the east is Doghouse Hill and Thorncombe Beacon; to the west is Lyme Bay stretching to the Devon distance but ahead lies Golden Cap, just a short climb across grassy land. The sheep who graze the fields below must have heads for heights and strong legs too. Maybe the view means nothing to them but for the stout shod who puff their way uphill the climb is amply rewarded.

Lyme Bay lies far below rimmed with white as the sea sucks and surges over the yellowy-grey shingle. Dark gorse clusters about the rocky scars of coastal inlets on the closed secret land. To stand on the Cap's blowy summit is to feel insignificant. It is so high you can look down on the birds. Lyme Regis winking in the glazed distance shows there is civilisation – but far away. When suburbia creeps ever onward and housing estates spread their greedy fingers into the soil it is reassuring to stand on Golden Cap, a last solitary, uninhabited stretch of England's 'green and pleasant land'.

Small craft, snug in Lyme Regis' harbour, point towards the 606 feet high Golden Cap in the distance. 'It is reassuring to stand on Golden Cap, a last solitary, uninhabited stretch of England.'

Kimmeridge

THERE are no bright lights, signposts or shining stars to guide you to a secret corner of Dorset's heart, only a modest little sign and a deep conviction that this is the right road.

Swanage side of Wareham a road runs through trees heavy with summer green, out towards the clear bright light that shows the sea is over the summit and Kimmeridge is waiting.

It is a little daunting perhaps, to be faced with red flags and dire warnings of military activity but having penetrated this far in the county's private life it seems unfair to turn around now. A wind-topped bluff looks out across a landscape that essentially hasn't changed in centuries. And while picnickers enjoy the alternate pleasures of tabloid tales and a flask of coffee they can imbibe an incomparable view. Seed laden grasses bend in the light, fresh air; so good you want to take great lungfuls and hold the memory for ever. On between deep, slow lanes and sleepy-eyed cows to the top of a hill and a painted wooden hut. It costs a few pence to intrude on a community's privacy and the pitted track drops down towards the sea and something unexpected.

Kimmeridge seems to be able to claim having done, had or got just about everything. But unlike a boastful third former Kimmeridge's tales are all true. Prehistory, history, industry, fishing,

A secret corner of Dorset's heart.

Thatched cottages line 'deep, slow lanes' on the way to Kimmeridge.

smuggling – even a stake in the twentieth century oil business. This once-thriving community can rightly talk of its past and its future. And to think it has all been played out around a stunning bay of clear, shallow water.

It is a privately-owned estate. For more than six centuries the land belonged to the Clavells and their descendants. Now it and 350-year-old Smedmor – the house – belongs to Major Mansel. The house itself is open to visitors on Wednesdays from June to September.

Kimmeridge Bay at first sight seems a little disappointing. Low grey shale cliffs, grey sand and shale beach, even through the water the dissected slabs of grey shale are clearly visible giving an impression of – well, grey. There's a lot more to it than first impressions though.

The sedimentary shale was laid down 150 million years ago and it is bursting with fossils – in fact Plesiosaurus and Ichthyosauras were cheerfully trotting around the bay a few million years back. The clear shallow water attracts a wealth of marine life which is now protected by the Purbeck Marine Life Reserve and can be explored with mask and flippers. In fact the bay is a diver's delight.

The Romans had a thriving trade here making jewellery from the shale and industry has continued through the centuries. At one time glass was made here; green glass bottles, beakers and wine goblets and in 1980/81 a glass furnace was excavated under what is now the boat park.

A lifeboat was stationed here from 1868 to 1896 but was finally abandoned because there was a chronic shortage of crew. And coast-

The church of St Michael and All Angels, Steeple, not many miles from Kimmeridge.

The way to Kimmeridge is like a trip into the past – Dorset at her most serene.

guards were kept on their toes here apprehending smugglers who obviously found it was easier to turn a dishonest penny.

But Kimmeridge's greatest wealth lies in its oil-bearing shale. Many fortunes have been lost trying to capitalise on the shales and other minerals found there. In fact during the nineteenth century a number of companies were started; some prospered for a while but in the end they all faltered. Lack of what nowadays is called infra-structure – communications, labour resources and so on – ultimately defeated them all. Gaulter Cottages, a row of houses at right-angles to the sea were built to house the shale miners but not even specialist housing could odds the problems until now.

The shale cliffs at Kimmeridge. Many fortunes have been lost trying to capitalise on Kimmeridge's oil bearing shale and other minerals.

A little nodding donkey pump steadily and methodically sucks 4.6 million gallons of oil each year from deep under Kimmeridge. It is a real success story for BP which even has plans to extend production.

Industry is certainly not to the forefront though. In fact this portion of land seems best part forgotten and tucked away from the rest of the world. The bay is dominated by the ruined Clavell tower built last century as a folly and then used as a coastguard lookout. Small yachts and dinghies skim the waters where once a fishing fleet plied its trade while further out on Kimmeridge Ledges ships have

The Clavell Tower at Kimmeridge.

been wrecked. The SS Treveal sank there in 1920. Her crew took to the lifeboats but these were swamped by icy seas. Of the 43 men who abandoned ship only seven were saved. The ship's toll of disaster did not stop there though. Other vessels have struck the wreck, one of which also sank.

On a hot summer's day it is hard to imagine tragedy, bankruptcy or indeed any of Kimmeridge's highs or lows of fortune – it is just Dorset at her most serene.

Quest for the truth

FACT and fiction have a habit of becoming hopelessly interwoven. Quite where the truth ends and the myth begins is often difficult to assess. And so it is with Fleet – the tiny Dorset village – and Meade Faulkner's *Moonfleet*, a rip-roaring tale of smugglers and adventure.

Fleet, perched above the salty lagoon at Chesil, is certainly the stuff that tales are made of. Snugly tucked away from passers-by down a road that defies two cars to pass at once, it has an aura of deeply held secrets.

Two churches, an imposing manor house and a history stretching back some seven thousand years is enough to make any community feel interesting. And that is without the added bonus of fleshing out the bones of a dramatic story that still captures the imagination of readers some 100 years after it was penned. Readers still walk along Butter Street – a charming row of old cottages – to find old Fleet Church and proof that the story of Moonfleet was true. But was it?

Victorian writer Meade Faulkner, like so many other men and women of literature, found inspiration in Dorset. Here were the characters, the communities, the light and shade of life ready to be blended into a tale so real that even a century later people still believe there was a Colonel John Mohune, that Squire Maskew lived and that Fleet House played host to treachery.

What Faulkner did was skilfully blend a mixture of features he knew in the parish with some he invented and some that were elsewhere in the county. A juxtaposition of names, much as Thomas Hardy did with his Wessex, completed the picture.

Old Fleet Church is a delight. A tiny, honey-coloured building surrounded by leaning gravestones it seems hard to believe that disaster has quite literally washed over its sacred ground. On November 23, 1824 a great storm swept through the village

A track winds its way through deep Dorset countryside.

destroying much of the village and part of the church. After the flood the new church was built and dedicated to the Holy Trinity by the Bishop of Bristol in 1829.

In fact the original Bridport to Weymouth road used to run right through the village of Fleet until the present main road, the B3157, was built. Quite how carriages and carts negotiated the track, that is now in parts footpath or bridleway, is difficult to comprehend.

Fleet clearly had its finger firmly on the pulse of history from the start. Dorsetmen back in the Stone Age were busy making tools and ornaments only a few yards from the old Church and the outlines of man's efforts to re-shape nature are clearly visible from the churchyard. Anglo-Saxons named the place *Floet* after the tidal lagoon there. After that a succession of owners held Fleet from Earl Harold in Edward the Confessor's time through to Henry VIII.

The old church at Fleet. Parts of it were swept away in a great storm in the 1820s.

The Mohun family who lived at Fleet House, where a country club now flourishes, provided valuable material for Meade Faulkner. He took the name *Mohun Fleet* for his novel and found the house itself a wonderful setting for a story. Of course there was more than a grain of truth in Fleet's smuggling links. In the eighteenth century three customs men met with a certain degree of hostility when they were sent off to investigate a reported landing of contraband at Fleet. A bloodthirsty crew, disguised and armed to the teeth, rapidly persuaded the trio to mind their own business.

The house itself has been inextricably linked to all that has happened in the parish over the years. Now the Moonfleet Manor Hotel, Fleet house has passed from Mohuns to Goulds, Jackson and Gooden until a retired Sherborne banker Alfred Pretor who rented the house, also felt moved by a literary bug. He wrote *Roland and I or*

The well cared-for interior of old Fleet Church.

The new church at Fleet built after a storm destroyed much of the old church.

Scenes and Characters from a Village of the Past and Fleet was immortalised in words once more.

Bristolian family the Georges owned the house when Meade Faulkner was researching his novel. No doubt he would have found it difficult to equate the gracious house and gardens of his day with that of half a century later. Fleet House was requisitioned during the 1939-45 war and in 1944 American troops moved in ready for the D-Day landings in Normandy.

Fleet has seen the pattern of life steadily unfold for thousands of years – different times and different people but essentially the same.

Dorset's special quality lies in her maternal calm, ready to embrace change and smooth over the rough edges until what is left is comfortable and loved. That is the magic of Dorset.

Rolling Dorset countryside.

Other Bossiney titles include

DORSET MYSTERIES
introduced by Jean Stubbs
Bossiney invites six authors to probe mysterious facets of Dorset.
'Dorset adds a final ingredient of its own – mystery.'

Margery Hull, Dorset Evening Echo

LEGENDS OF DORSET
by Polly Lloyd
The author explores legendary Dorset, visiting places as diverse as the Sacred Circle at Knowlton and Chesil Beach. Dorset is a mine of myth and folklore.
'Weird happenings . . . Polly Lloyd delves through tales ranging from moving rocks to murders . . .'

Ed Perkins, Southern Evening Echo

GHOSTS OF DORSET
by Peter Underwood
The President of the Ghost Club explores a whole range of Dorset hauntings. A ghostly white donkey, a world-famous screaming skull, phantom coach-and-horses story which Thomas Hardy used in *Tess of the D'Urbervilles* and a prehistoric 'Peeping Tom' are some of the subjects.
Ghost hunter Peter Underwood has been spook stalking in Dorset uncovering a host of eerie brushes with the Supernatural.'

Bournemouth Advertiser

SUPERNATURAL ADVENTURE
by Michael Williams
Contains a great deal of unpublished material relating to the Supernatural.
'Spiritual healing, automatic writing are just a few of the spectrum of subjects . . . neat, well-presented . . . easy-to-read volume.'

Psychic News

WESTCOUNTRY MYSTERIES
Introduced by Colin Wilson
A team of authors probes mysterious happenings in Somerset, Devon and Cornwall. Drawings and photographs all add to the mysterious content.
'A team of authors has joined forces to re-examine and probe various yarns from the puzzling to the tragic.'

Also available

BOSSINEY'S FIRST WILTSHIRE TITLES are:

WILTSHIRE MYSTERIES
Introduced by David Foot

GHOSTS OF WILTSHIRE
by Peter Underwood, President of The Ghost Club

OTHER RECENT TITLES include:

ABOUT EXMOOR
by Polly Lloyd

DEVON CURIOSITIES
by Jane Langton

SAINTS OF THE SOUTH WEST
by James Mildren

UNKNOWN SOMERSET
by Rosemary Clinch and Michael Williams

DAPHNE DU MAURIER COUNTRY
by Martyn Shallcross

KING ARTHUR IN SOMERSET
by Rosemary Clinch and Michael Williams

HIDDEN KNOWLEDGE
by Lori Reid

THE QUANTOCKS
by Julia Davey

PLYMOUTH IN WAR AND PEACE
by Guy Fleming

We shall be pleased to send you our catalogue giving full details of our growing list of titles for Devon, Cornwall, Dorset, Somerset and Wiltshire and forthcoming publications. If you have difficulty in obtaining our titles, write direct to Bossiney Books, Land's End, St Teath, Bodmin, Cornwall.